I Want YOU...

To Succeed In Your Corporate Climb

How My Common Sense Coaching Can Help You
Create the Corporate Career Success
You Want and Deserve

Bud Bilanich

The Common Sense Guy

Table of Contents

Chapter 1: How to Use This Book

"Whatever you vividly imagine, ardently desire, sincerely believe and enthusiastically act upon... must inevitably come to pass."

—*Paul J. Meyer*

Success! That's what I offer you — personal and professional success. By reading this book, you'll get to know:

- How to become a personal and professional success;

- The kinds of help you can get from me;

- How I deliver it;

- Who I am and why you should trust me;

- Your options; and how to decide what to do next.

I recommend you get a highlighter or pen. Scan the table of contents, and flip to whatever catches your interest. Then go back to the beginning, and read the entire book all the way through.

As you scan and read mark anything that strikes you. Use the "Questions" page at the very end of the book to list things you'd like to ask me. Then when

3

you are ready, call me at 303 393 0446; or email me at Bud@BudBilanich.com

Chapter 2: The Challenges of Becoming a Personal and Professional Success

I am a woman in process. I'm just trying like everybody else. I try to take every conflict and every experience and learn from it. Life is never dull.

Oprah Winfrey

In the course of my coaching career, I have worked with a number of highly successful people — C level execs, VPs, directors, managers, individual contributors, and young people just starting out. I am honored to say that they have told me that I made a meaningful contribution to their success. I think they succeeded because they were persistent in pursuing their success. They learned from their experiences. They did what they had to do, including getting the help they needed to succeed.

The five stories below are indicative of one of the points I always make in my talks, my writing and my coaching. Good performance alone will not lead to success.

All successful people are outstanding performers, but not all outstanding performers are successful people. Read that sentence again. It is at the heart of my philosophy on personal and professional success.

5

If you want to succeed, you need to not only be a good performer, you need to be self confident, create positive personal impact, communicate effectively and be interpersonally competent.

Don't take my word for it. Read the five stories below. They are the true stories of five of my coaching clients...

Susan's Story

Susan is a great business development professional. She has an uncanny ability to identify and build strong relationships with potential partners for her company. She is good at closing deals.

A while back, she called me to discuss an opportunity. She was being aggressively recruited by another company in her industry. This company wanted her to become their VP of Business Development. She would be running their business development function, with several people reporting to her. She wanted my advice.

As we spoke, Susan said that she was flattered to be recruited so heavily, but worried that she might not be up to the task if she took the job. She said that she knew she is good at what she does, but she hadn't managed people for quite a while and wasn't sure she would succeed as the head of a business development group.

At the end of our conversation, Susan realized that her fear of failing was keeping her from considering a great career opportunity. Fear is the enemy of self confidence. Susan's lack of self confidence, because of her fear of failure, was keeping her from considering a plum job.

Once she realized this, Susan decided to face her fear and act. She accepted the job and became a great success at it.

Susan's story illustrates one of the keys to success on which I work with my coaching clients. Successful people are self confident. They are optimistic. They face their fears and deal with them. They surround themselves with positive people.

Bob's Story

Bob retired recently as the VP of Compensation and Benefits for a Fortune 50 company. By all accounts, he had a very successful career, but one that almost didn't get started because of his poor personal impact.

Bob began his working life as a teacher. He wore short sleeved shirts and jeans or khakis to school every day. However, Bob found teaching unrewarding, so he went to school at night to get an MA in Human Resources Management. Because he was a teacher, he had the opportunity to do a summer internship.

He applied for several, and got one. After he completed his MA, the company for whom he did the internship hired him. But all of this almost didn't happen; because of the way Bob was dressed for his internship interview.

Bob arrived for his intern interview dressed in a polyester sport coat, with a short sleeved shirt, light colored polyester slacks and walking shoes. This was the 1980's in New York City. In those days, business men wore dark colored wool suits, white or light blue shirts, foulard ties and wing tip shoes. Bob stood out like a sore thumb. He interviewed well, but almost didn't get the internship because one of the VPs thought that he didn't have a professional image.

Bob spent the summer working at his internship. His boss thought that Bob would realize that he looked different from most people at the company and buy some different clothes. He didn't. Finally, toward the end of his internship, Bob's boss asked me to work with him on developing a more professional and polished look.

Bob was floored. He had received all sorts of praise for the work he had done as an intern. He had performed very well. But his boss was telling him, through me, that he might not be offered a job when he graduated because of what he wore.

Bob bought himself a few dark wool suits, several white shirts, foulard ties and a pair of wing tips. The

Learn more and get some great free success helpers:
http://BudBilanich.com/success.html

next spring, he was offered a job at his internship company, where he had nothing short of a meteoric rise to VP of Comp and Benefits.

Bob's story illustrates another key to success. Successful people create positive personal impact. They build and nurture a strong personal brand. They dress well, and appropriately, for their situation. They understand and use the basic rules of business etiquette.

Sandy's Story

Sandy is the VP of Sales for a division of a Fortune 50 company. She began her career with the company right out of college. She accepted a sales job and was placed in a territory that was considered to be one of the worst performing territories in the company. This didn't stop Sandy. She set a goal of increasing the previous year's sales by 50%. This was an ambitious goal. Her quota called for her to reach 110% of the previous year's sales.

Sandy became an expert in her company's products. She also became an expert in the products offered by her competitors. Every night, she spent an hour with a map planning out her call route for the next day. As she drove from call to call, she listened to motivational and sales success cd's and tapes.

Sandy reached her goal of 150% of previous year's sales. She set a similar goal for the following year.

Learn more and get some great free success helpers:
http://BudBilanich.com/success.html

She reached that goal too. In her first five years, Sandy always set, and reached, goals that were higher than her quota. But she couldn't seem to take the next step. She always came up short when it came time to be promoted to District Manager.

Sandy called her manager and asked for some candid feedback on why she kept getting passed over for promotions, even though she was one of the top performing sales people in the company. He told her that she wasn't seen as a team player. He encouraged her to work with a coach to improve her teamwork skills.

Sandy worked with me. During our work together, she came to see that at times she ran roughshod over her colleagues. Many of them didn't like working with her. With my help, she learned how to become a better team player. She put this knowledge to work. She got her promotion to District Manager.

Her District quickly became the highest performing District in the company. After a few years, Sandy was named Regional Sales Director and then went on to become the first woman VP of Sales in her company.

Sandy attributed some of her success to the things she learned while working a territory; challenge yourself by setting high goals, plan your day then work your plan, make the most of your time. However, to this day, she attributes most of her success to what she learned during our time working together. Being a good performer is not enough to guarantee success. Other, seemingly little factors — like building strong relationships with coworkers — are important too.

Sandy's story illustrates another key to success: outstanding performance. Outstanding performers are technically competent. They are technically competent because they are lifelong learners. They set high goals, and achieve them. They are organized. They manage their time, life and stress well. And, they realize that outstanding performance is not enough for long term, lasting success.

Pat's Story

Pat was very good at her job. So good in fact, that she was asked to make a presentation to the President of her Division and his direct reports on a project that she had brought in on time and under budget.

Pat knew this was a big opportunity to strut her stuff for senior management. She spent hours writing and rewriting her presentation. Then she memorized it. She was confident that she would do a great talk and be on her way to a promotion and even more success.

However, Pat made the mistake of assuming that the President wanted all of the details of her project. She put together a 45 minute presentation. Her PowerPoint slides went into great detail.

A few minutes into her talk, the Division President said, "Pat, we don't need all of these details, please give us a high level overview. We allowed only 15 minutes for your presentation. We have only 10 minutes left."

That knocked Pat for a loop. She had memorized her talk, and had real difficulty in deviating from it. She went right back to saying what she had practiced, not what the President had asked her to do.

After a few minutes, Pat's boss stepped in, and presented the highlights of her project, somewhat saving the day. Pat however, was devastated. She thought she had blown her one chance to make an impression with the President and his direct reports.

She came to me for some coaching on how to become a better presenter. I worked with her closely. One of the tips I gave her right at the start was to always make sure she understood what the audience wanted and expected from her presentation. If she had done this prior to her talk for the Division President, she wouldn't have prepared and memorized a 45 minute talk. She would have come up with something shorter that hit the highlights of her project.

Pat got a second chance. By then, she had worked hard at becoming an excellent presenter. She wowed the President and his direct reports in her next talk, and eventually got the promotion that propelled her to a great career in her company.

Pat's story also illustrates another key to success. Successful people have excellent communication skills. They are great conversationalists. They write clearly and succinctly. They make great presentations; to groups of two or two hundred.

James' Story

James was with his company for close to 30 years and was a very senior executive. He had risen through the ranks and was well regarded by almost everyone who knew him. Recently, he was asked to resign.

James became the protégé of a senior manager early on. As the manager moved up, James moved up with him. The manager had great faith in James' business acumen and his problem solving ability. Whenever a problem arose, James' manager asked him to "look into it and fix it."

James enjoyed these challenges. He was smart, and had an uncanny ability to zero in on what was going wrong. He was equally adept at coming up with solutions to problems.

Learn more and get some great free success helpers:
http://BudBilanich.com/success.html

James had a problem though. Most of the time, the problems he was asked to fix were not in his area of responsibility. They were problems that his peers, other people at his level, who reported to his boss, were experiencing. In pleasing his boss and solving problems, James stepped all over the toes of his peers. They came to resent him for it.

One day, his boss left the company. One of James' peers was appointed to take his place. Three months later, James was asked to resign. He was asked to resign not because of his performance. In some ways, it was because he was too competent. He was asked to resign because he hadn't built strong relationships with his peers. Often, by doing what his boss wanted, he alienated the people closest to him.

James and I began working together on his interpersonal skills. James came to understand that it was important not only to do a great job and to fix problems, but to do so in a way that did not alienate those around him.

I'm happy to say that James landed a job as President of a small company in his industry. We still speak. He tells me that the secret to his newfound success is his willingness to work hard to build and maintain relationships with people at all levels of his company.

James' story illustrates one final point about success. Successful people are interpersonally

14

competent. They understand themselves. They use this self awareness to better understand other people and how to be influential with them. They build and nurture strong relationships. They resolve conflict with a minimal amount of upset to their relationships.

Do any of these stories sound familiar to you? Maybe you're a Susan, Bob, Sandy, Pat or James. Maybe you have something else holding you back.

Regardless, these five stories illustrate one important point about career and life success. It takes more than good performance to become a personal and professional success. It takes a combination of self confidence, positive personal impact, outstanding performance, communication skills and interpersonal competence to succeed in your career and life. People who are successful in their lives and careers have mastered all of these five elements, and excel in one or two of them.

In my work as a success coach I have found that the single biggest career success mistake that people make is assuming that competence and performance are their ticket to success, when in fact they are merely the price of admission. Most people are good performers. It's a huge mistake to think that good performance is the only element of a successful career.

Learn more and get some great free success helpers:
http://BudBilanich.com/success.html

Outstanding performance is very important to career and life success. It's at the heart of the five success elements. No one can be successful without being a highly competent, outstanding performer. The incompetents and poor performers get identified and asked to leave or are placed in marginal positions pretty quickly.

However, don't forget the other four success factors. You have to be self confident, make a positive personal impact, have highly developed communication skills and act in an interpersonally competent manner if you are going to succeed. These four elements are necessary complements to outstanding performance.

I help my coaching clients identify which of these areas are a strength for them and in which areas they need to improve. I can help you identify and bypass your personal roadblocks.

Chapter 3: The Power of Coaching

Surround yourself with positive people and situations and avoid negativity.

Doreen Virtue

The will to win is important. But the will to prepare is vital.

Joe Paterno

Coaching is a partnership; a creative and thought-provoking process that will inspire you to be all that you can be — to live up to your full personal and professional potential. Coaches, by definition, are positive people. We derive tremendous satisfaction from seeing others succeed.

As a coach, I've been trained to listen, to observe, and to customize my approach to your individual needs. My job is to provide the support you need to enhance the skills, resources, and creativity that you already have. I'll work hard to elicit solutions and strategies from you. I believe that you are naturally creative and resourceful. I'll bring out your creativity and resourcefulness.

Together we will create a powerful and ongoing partnership designed to help you produce fulfilling results in your personal and professional life. My goal is to help you improve your performance — and enhance the quality of your life.

Thanks for reading this far. Here are some questions that you may be wondering about at this juncture.

What exactly do I do as a coach?

Good question. As a coach I:

- Provide you with a framework for accountability.

- Help you identify, clarify and achieve your goals.

- Help you reframe your beliefs in ways that are consistent with your goals.

How does coaching differ from therapy, consulting, sports coaching, or having a supportive friend?

- Coaching is not therapy. Therapy seeks to bring awareness and understanding of the past to a client. As your coach, I will provide the support and strategy to help you make changes based on your present awareness and your desires for the future.

18

- There are many approaches to coaching. In general, coaching is not unlike consulting. However, consulting addresses specific problems by offering solutions. I prefer to develop and nurture ongoing coaching relationships where I will stay with you as you implement new skills, changes in your behavior, and work towards your goals. In general, I find that my coaching clients and I both know when it is time to end our coaching relationship.

  Consulting often involves dispensing advice, telling people what they should do. While my coaching will focus on assisting you to discover your own solutions, I will offer my advice when you ask for it, and when I think it is necessary.

- Coaching employs several principles from sports coaching — for example, teamwork, and monitoring and exceeding performance, in order to be one's best. However, unlike sports coaching, you and I will not be focused on winning or losing. Instead, our focus will be on strengthening your skills.

- A supportive friend is wonderful to have, yet can seldom provide the objectivity and distance that a coach does. As a coach, I'm a professional. You can trust me to work with you on the most important aspects of your life or business. I will offer you a different perspective than your friends because ours will be a professional relational that affords us both the value of emotional distance.

Who hires a coach?

- Corporations have hired me to coach executives, leaders, high potential employees, underperforming individuals and teams.

- Small business people and entrepreneurs have hired me to help them with a variety of tasks, from goal setting to strategic planning to dealing with suppliers and vendors to managing their workforce.

- Individuals have hired me to provide them with coaching related to career and life success.

I have found that most individuals hire me for similar reasons:

- They want more — more success, better performance, more satisfaction, more balance, more money, more peace, better relationships.

- They want to grow in all aspects of their lives and be productive.

- They want to discover innovative ways to do things effortlessly.

Do I work on personal goals, or on business and professional goals with my clients?

The answer is "Both." My coaching is most valuable when I work with all aspects of personal, business, and professional goals relating to who you are and what you want.

What is the focus of my coaching?

I will focus where you need me most. Some of the questions that I might help you address include:

- What are your goals? Are they based in your values?

- Where are you now in relation to where you want to be?

- In order to get what you want from any situation, what are the areas of strength and what are the areas for improvement and focus?

By creating the focus of coaching around what you want to achieve, I will help you maintain focus on that which will make you most successful — personally and professionally.

Why does my coaching work?

My coaching works for several reasons:

- The synergy between us creates positive momentum.

- We will set well-defined goals for our work together. I will support you as you move toward reaching your goals.

- You will develop new skills, which will translate into more success and a balanced life.

Why has coaching become so popular?

Several reasons:

- Many people are tired of doing what they think they *should* do and are ready to do what they *want* to do.

- People realize that now they can accomplish things that might have felt out of reach just a few years ago. More people are investing in their personal and professional growth.

- Spirituality. People are seeking deeper meaning in their lives and work. Companies are seeking innovative ways to grow themselves from the inside out, to harmonize their goals and their employees' goals.

Chapter 4: What Coaching is NOT

Success is a choice. You must decide what you want, why you want it and how you plan to achieve it. No one else can, will or should do that for you.

Gary Ryan Blair

Sometimes it is easier to understand a concept such as coaching in terms of what it is *not*. Here are some contrasts to coaching:

- Coaching is not therapy. Therapy deals with the past, with what was broken, and how to fix it. My coaching deals with the present and the future, with what is right, and how to make it more right. The goal of therapy is to take you from "broken" to "functional." My coaching will help you go from "functional" to "extraordinary."

- Coaching is not consulting. Consulting brings to bear best practices and subject-matter knowledge on a situation. In my coaching, I assume that you have many of the answers inside you. I will focus on asking you the right questions to help you find your own solutions. I will offer advice and suggestions only after we have exhausted your own thoughts and ideas.

- Coaching is not mentoring. Mentors seek to provide guidance and solutions to clients based on their own experiences. In my coaching, I will help you apply your experience and wisdom to your present needs.

As I mentioned above, I will give advice, and bring my knowledge of personal and professional success to bear on your situation. But I will do so in a manner that assumes you have a lot of the answers to how to become a personal and professional success.

Chapter 5: My "Secret Sauce"

If you have only a hammer, every problem looks like a nail. Successful people have a complete toolbox at their disposal — and they use all of the tools.

Bud Bilanich

"So Bud, what's so special about you and your coaching?"

That's a great question and one you should ask if you're considering working with me.

I've spent my entire working life in the people development field — the first 15 as a trainer for some very large US companies and the last 20 as a success coach, motivational speaker and author and blogger.

I've built a million dollar business from scratch. I've written three books on personal success and four on how to run a successful business. I received an EdD (Doctor of Education) from Harvard.

I've coached all kinds of people at different stages of their careers: C level executives, Vice Presidents, Directors, Managers and individual contributors.

Most important, I'm passionate about helping other people achieve the personal and professional success they want and deserve.

I've been studying success and successful people for over 20 years. During that time, I've developed my recipe for success. It has four main ingredients:

- Clarity
- Commitment
- Confidence
- Competence

Below I discuss each of these in some detail. I encourage you to take notes as you read. There is a place for questions at the end of this book. Jot down any questions you may have about my secret sauce and how it can help you become a personal and professional success.

Clarity

Clarity of purpose and direction is fundamental to your professional success. It all begins with a clear picture of how you define professional success.

When I was 25, if you asked me what I wanted to be doing when I was 50, I would have told you, "Running a one person consulting, coaching and speaking business from my house." Guess what? I have been running a one person consulting, coaching and speaking business from my house ever since 1988. My clarity of purpose propelled me toward my goal.

I have a friend who is a serial entrepreneur. He started a software business when he was 27. He built it up and sold it to a major computer manufacturer by the time he was 35. He has since started and sold four other companies. His clarity of purpose lies in the challenge of creating something new, building it into a viable, sustainable business and then moving on.

I have another friend who recently retired as the Executive VP of Human Resources for a Fortune 50 company. We were chatting a few days ago. She told me that when she was in college, she decided that she was going to join a good company and work her way up the ladder. She took an entry level HR job with a company she liked. It took her over 25 years, but she eventually became the most senior HR person in that company. Her clarity of purpose and definition of success was different from mine, but she reached her goal.

My second friend told me that her son has yet a different definition of success. He is not interested in climbing the corporate ladder, or in being an entrepreneur. He wants an interesting job where he can contribute, but he doesn't want to spend inordinate amounts of time at work. He wants to spend as much time with his family as he can. His definition of success is different from his mother's.

All four of us are professional successes – according to our clarity of purpose.

There is no one correct definition of professional success. There are as many definitions as there are people in this world. Your definition of professional success is what's right for you — not anyone else. I would not have been happy building and selling a number of businesses in succession, climbing a corporate ladder or working for a large company in an individual contributor position. However, as you can tell from the stories of the three people above, they were. They knew what they wanted and they went after it.

That's why defining your clarity of purpose is so important. Your clarity of purpose provides both a foundation and launching pad for your professional success. The old saying, "If you don't know where you're going, you won't know when you get there" is a cliché but true. Getting clear on your personal definition of professional success is the first step to becoming a career and life success.

If you haven't already done so, I suggest you take some time and think about your clarity of purpose. How do you define professional success for yourself? Keep that purpose and definition of success in mind as you read the other rules in this book. Think about how these rules can help you reach your purpose.

Commitment

It's simple, really. Success is all up to you, and me, and anyone else who wants it. We all have to take personal responsibility for our own success. I am the only one who can make me a success. You are the only one who can make you a success.

Stuff happens: good stuff, bad stuff, frustrating stuff, unexpected stuff. Successful people respond to the stuff that happens in a positive way. Humans are the only animals with free will. That means we — you and me — get to decide how we react to every situation that comes up. That's why committing to taking personal responsibility for your personal and professional success is so important.

Personal responsibility means recognizing that you are responsible for your life and the choices you make. It means that you realize that while other people and events have an impact on your life, these people and events don't shape your life. When you accept personal responsibility for your life, you own up to the fact that how you react to people and events is what's important. And you can choose how to react to every person you meet and everything that happens to you.

The concept of personal responsibility is found in most writings on success. Stephen Covey's first of the seven habits of highly effective people is, "Be proactive." My friend John Miller's book *QBQ: the Question Behind the Question* asks readers to pose questions like, "What can I do to become a top performer?" John really believes that taking personal responsibility for your life and career is the key to professional success.

The other two keys to success — confidence and competence — work only if you are willing to take responsibility for your life and career. Commitment to personal responsibility is the foundation on which this model is built.

Personal responsibility means using this material once you learn it. I've written this book to provide you with useful information and knowledge on becoming a professional success. But, as the U.S. Steel pencils my Dad brought home from work used to say, "Knowing is not enough."

When I was a kid, I was really fascinated and puzzled by these pencils. "Knowing is not enough — what the hell does that mean?" I used to think. I spent hours struggling with that idea. I was too stubborn to ask a grown-up.

When I got to Penn State, I took Philosophy 101 my freshman year. We had to read Johann von Goethe. One day, as I was plowing through an assignment, I came across this quote: "Knowing is not enough, we must do. Willing is not enough, we must apply."

Boy was I glad I took that course! It solved one of the profound mysteries of my childhood: "Knowing is not enough." As I take it, you have to take what you learn and use it, or what you've learned isn't very valuable. That's part of personal responsibility, using your knowledge to achieve your goals.

Confidence

I love stories. I think they are a very powerful way of making important points. Here's one of my favorites about self confidence.

> The business executive was deep in debt and could see no way out. Creditors were closing in on him. Suppliers were demanding payment. He sat on the park bench, head in hands, wondering if anything could save his company from bankruptcy.
>
> Suddenly an old man appeared before him. "I can see that something is troubling you," he said. After listening to the executive's woes, the old man said, "I believe I can help you." He asked the man his name, wrote out a check, and pushed it into his hand saying, "Take this money. Meet me here exactly one year from today, and you can pay me back at that time."

Learn more and get some great free success helpers:
http://BudBilanich.com/success.html

Then he turned and disappeared as quickly as he had come.

The business executive saw in his hand a check for $500,000, signed by John D. Rockefeller, then one of the richest men in the world! "I can erase my money worries in an instant!" he realized. But instead, the executive decided to put the uncashed check in his safe.

Just knowing it was there might give him the strength to work out a way to save his business. With renewed optimism, he negotiated better deals and extended terms of payment. He closed several big sales. Within a few months, he was out of debt and making money once again.

Exactly one year later, he returned to the park with the uncashed check. At the agreed-upon time, the old man appeared. But just as the executive was about to hand back the check and share his success story, a nurse came running up and grabbed the old man.

"I'm so glad I caught him!" she cried. "I hope he hasn't been bothering you. He's always escaping from the rest

Learn more and get some great free success helpers:
http://BudBilanich.com/success.html

home and telling people he's John D. Rockefeller." And she led the old man away by the arm.

The astonished executive just stood there, stunned. All year long he'd been wheeling and dealing, buying and selling, convinced he had half a million dollars behind him. Suddenly, he realized that it wasn't the money, real or imagined, that had turned his life around. It was his newfound self-confidence that gave him the power to achieve anything he went after.

As nice as this story is, I doubt if it is actually true. However, like a lot of fables, it makes a great common sense point about personal and professional success. If you believe in yourself and your success, you are likely to find ways to make that belief come true. Think about it.

If you want to become self confident you need to do three things. 1) Become an optimist. Learn from, and then forget yesterday's mistakes. Focus on tomorrow's achievements. 2) Face your fears and take action. Action cures fear. Procrastination and inaction compound it. Failure is rarely fatal. Do something, anything that will move you closer to achieving your goals. 3) Surround yourself with positive people. Build a network of supportive friends. Jettison the negative people in your life.

Competence

If you want to succeed in this life, you have to be competent. You need to develop a universal set of skills. These skills are:

- Creating Positive Personal Impact,
- Performing in an Outstanding Manner,
- Communication,
- Interpersonal Competence.

Let's take a look at each of these skills sets...

Positive Personal Impact

All successful people create positive personal impact. Positive personal impact is like charisma, only more so. People gravitate towards people with positive personal impact. When you create positive personal impact other people want to be around you. They want to work with you. They want to be your friend.

People with positive personal impact develop and nurture their personal brand. They are impeccable in their presentation of self. They know and follow the basic rules of etiquette. If you master these three keys, you'll be able to create positive personal impact.

I have a model of customer service that I use with my consulting clients. It begins from the premise that after any interaction your customers rate you.

The people in your life R.A.T.E. you too. You can use your R.A.T.E.ing to build positive personal impact. It works like this...

- R stands for Responsiveness;
- A stands for Assurance;
- T stands for Tangibles; and
- E stands for Empathy.

If you notice, only one of the four points in the model — tangibles — is what you actually do for or deliver to the people in your life. The other three are the emotional measures by which people judge you. These emotional measures are at least as important as the tangibles you deliver, especially when it comes to creating positive personal impact.

You have to deliver the tangibles. You must produce results. That's the cost of a ticket to the personal and professional success sweepstakes.

However, you have to pay attention to the other three factors — responsiveness, assurance, and empathy – if you're going to make a positive personal impact while you're performing. Let's look at each of these three in detail.

Responsiveness — You have to ensure that the people in your life see you as someone who is willing to help, someone who understands what needs to be done and is willing to do it. Other people need to think that you will give them what they want, when they want it, and in a manner that they can use it.

Assurance — You have to be able to convey trust and confidence. People need to feel that you are going to deliver. To do this, you must be very knowledgeable about the people in your life and their needs and wants. You need to be clear on what you can offer them to help them meet their goals. You need to ensure that they are confident that you will do what you say you will do.

Empathy — The people in your life must perceive you as an individual who understands, cares about, and pays attention to their needs. To do this, you need to be willing to walk a mile in your customers' shoes. You have to demonstrate to them that you are aware of and sensitive to their unique and individual needs.

The common sense point here is simple. To make a positive personal impact, you must do more than deliver results, look good, and act graciously. You have to be seen by others as a person who is responsive to their requests. You have to build trust with these individuals, and you need to demonstrate that you understand their needs and issues.

Outstanding Performance

All successful people are outstanding performers. It's the price of admission to the success club. However, don't make the mistake of thinking that performance alone will get you where you want to go. Performance is but one of the seven characteristics of successful people. Performance is important, but it alone will not guarantee your success.

There are several common sense points associated with outstanding performance. First, become a lifelong learner. Keep learning and growing. Second, set high goals — and then meet or exceed them. Use milestones to break your goals into manageable chunks. They'll be easier to achieve this way. Third, get organized. This will help you manage your life, time and stress. Figure out an organizing system that works for you and stick with it.

When it comes to outstanding performance, one of my favorite quotes comes from Louis Pasteur, the inventor of the pasteurization process and widely considered the father of modern microbiology. I really like what he has to say about tenacity: "Let me tell you the secret that has led me to my goal: my strength lies solely in my tenacity."

Here's a story about a tenacious person who is very close to me. My wife, Cathy, is a volunteer reading tutor at one of Denver's public schools. She's been doing this for several years now. She enjoys the children, and she feels that she is making a difference through her volunteer work.

As August turns into September, she always gets excited about another school year and another group of kids. One year, the school where she volunteers lost its Volunteer Program Coordinator, so they were a little slow getting volunteer assignments done. This didn't stop Cathy. She made a few phone calls to the school asking when they wanted her to begin. She got some vague promises but nothing definite. Finally, she went to the school and basically arranged her own assignment. As usual, she loved the kids and was happy to be back at "her school."

The common sense point of the Pasteur quote and Cathy's tenacity in her volunteer work is simple. Outstanding performers are tenacious in pursuing their goals. They do what it takes to be successful. In Cathy's case, it took driving to the school and being willing to seem like a bit of a pain in the butt to an administrator. However, she was willing to do that because her desire to succeed as a reading volunteer was strong. The third graders with whom she reads are better off for it.

Remember Cathy's story the next time you run into a frustrating obstacle. Be tenacious. You'll be surprised at how often you'll reach your goal.

The Dalai Lama has some interesting things to say about outstanding performance. " One can be deceived by three types of laziness: the laziness of indolence, which is the wish to procrastinate; the laziness of inferiority, which is doubting your capabilities; and the laziness that is attached to negative actions, or putting great effort into non-virtue."

I really like this quote because it drives home an important point about taking personal responsibility for becoming an outstanding performer. The Dalai Lama doesn't let us off the hook by saying, "I didn't think I could do it." Instead, he says that doubting our abilities is a form of laziness. That's some tough love!

And, if you think about it, he is right. All too often, we let ourselves off the hook by saying, "I'm not going to try that, because I don't think I can do it." This is being lazy. "I can't do it, so I won't even try." As I read these words out loud, they sound pretty lame. Agree? If you do, you'll stop using lack of self confidence as an excuse for not doing the work it takes to become an outstanding performer.

Dynamic Communication

The life of a business traveler, especially one like me who travels to New York City regularly, appears glamorous at first glance. People always ask me if

I've eaten at famous restaurants like 21 or the latest hot spot they've read about in *Travel and Leisure.*

Most often when I'm in New York and don't have a business dinner, I dine on Chinese food delivered to my hotel room from the Cottage Noodle Shop. I've never even been in this restaurant, even though I have eaten their food at least 100 times. I am particularly fond of the Cottage Noodle Shop's Hot and Sour Soup, Vegetable Dumplings, and Lo Mein. If you're ever in New York, check them out. They're in the 40s on Ninth Avenue.

Once when I ordered from the Cottage Noodle Shop, my fortune cookie read, "Your talents will be recognized and suitably rewarded." I was happy with this fortune, but it made me think.

My talents, your talents, everyone's talents will be recognized and rewarded if we develop and use our communication skills. There are three types of communication skills critically important for career and life success: 1) Conversation skills; 2) Writing skills; and 3) Presentation skills.

You need to develop each of these skills if you want to have your talents recognized.

There are a few common sense points associated with becoming a dynamic communicator. Become a good conversationalist by listening. Take an active interest in other people and what they're saying. Show them you're listening by asking appropriate follow up questions to what they say. Write in a manner that communicates well. In general, this means being clear, concise and easily readable. The best way to make sure your writing is readable is to read it aloud before sending it. Finally, preparation is the most important key to doing a good presentation. If you follow the five steps I've laid out above, you'll be able to develop and present great talks.

Communication skills are not just for entrepreneurs. Here's an example of how my communication skills helped me get noticed when I was working for a very large company in the 1980's. One day I happened to get on an elevator with the president of the largest and most profitable division in the company. I was going to be conducting a workshop at his division's upcoming national sales meeting. I introduced myself to him and told him that I was looking forward to his sales meeting. We chatted briefly in the elevator and for a few minutes when we got to the lobby. He invited me to his office to talk some more. As a result of that conversation, I became a leadership consultant to him and his leadership team.

Dynamic communication skills are also important for building your professional network. Networking is an important but often overlooked communication skill. It is helpful when you are looking for a job, but it is even more important when you are happy with your situation. All people who are professional successes build and nurture strong networks.

Networking is an important skill. Successful people have large networks. They have people they can call on to help them. They know they can call on these people because these people know they can call on them. That's the real secret of networking — look to help others, not just to find out how they can help you.

Writing is another necessary tool that helps get your skills noticed. When I was in high school, I was the editor of my yearbook. To raise funds to cover the cost of our yearbook, we sold ads. There were a lot of factories in the town where I grew up. In the past, the yearbook staff had never approached these factories to place ads in the yearbook. I wrote sales letters to all of the plant managers. We got several full page ads from those letters.

One of the plant managers wrote back, asking if I would come to see him. I got dressed up in my one and only suit and went to his office at the appointed time. When I arrived, his secretary buzzed him to let him know I was there. I heard her say, "No, sir, he sent a student." When I walked in to his office and introduced myself, he was surprised. He told me that my sales letter was so well written that he thought I was the teacher who was the yearbook sponsor.

Two years later, I was looking for a summer job after my first year of college. The market was tight. I called this man. He remembered me, and I got a job.

Presentation skills may present the biggest opportunity for getting your talents noticed. As I have always worked in training and development, I had to develop and hone my presentation skills at a young age. This wasn't too difficult for me because I never suffered from stage fright. I used to compete in speech contests when I was in high school. I was the emcee for my high school talent show. I was on the radio in college.

Just a few months ago, I did a talk for a local chamber of commerce. As it so happens, the Sheriff's department is a member of this chamber. The Sheriff himself happened to be there that day. He liked my talk. About a week later, I got a call from his training officer. The Sheriff asked him to get in touch with me to conduct some supervisory training for their sergeants. I never would have gotten this business if it weren't for the notice I received from a talk at that chamber meeting.

Interpersonal Competence

Interpersonal competence is the fifth key of career and life success. No matter how self confident you are, how good you are at creating positive personal impact, how great a performer or dynamic a communicator you are, you will not succeed if you are not interpersonally competent.

Pat Wiesner is a friend. He is the publisher of
Colorado Business. A while back he wrote a great
column entitled "The Biggest Management Sin of
All: How to Lose Your Job or at least Deserve to
Lose It."

The biggest sin? Demeaning people. Pat says, "My
belief is that if we get caught shouting at people,
demeaning them in any way, we should be fired. On
the spot."

I agree. And this holds for everyone — not just
people in leadership and management positions.
Raising your voice and demeaning people is not
only poor leadership, it is one of the hallmarks of
interpersonally incompetent people.

Belittling, intimidating, or otherwise demeaning
people is not only nasty, it is destructive to their self
esteem and self confidence. Pat says, "Once you
have made someone feel really negative about
himself, how long would it take to reverse that
feeling? Pretty tough to do." Interpersonally
competent people help others build — not destroy
— their self confidence.

Interpersonally incompetent people often seem to
feel that the best way to feel good about themselves
is to make others feel bad about themselves. That's
why they often engage in demeaning and bullying
behavior.

This is simply not true. The title of one of the first self-help books I ever read — published by Thomas Harris in 1969, *I'm OK, You're OK* — says it best. Interpersonally competent people come from an "I'm OK, You're OK" place. Bullies and demeaning people come from an "I'm OK, You're Not OK" place.

Interpersonally competent people realize that we're all OK. They work hard to meet people where they are and to build strong relationships with all of the people in their lives.

Treat people with kindness and respect. Help them enhance their feelings of self esteem. Do what you can to build their self confidence. If you do, you'll be known as an interpersonally competent person — and interpersonally competent people are welcome wherever they go.

Interpersonal competence will help you create rich relationships that last a lifetime. In *The Little Black Book of Connections*, Jeffrey Gitomer offers the best piece of common sense advice I've ever seen when it comes to relationships:

> "Everyone wants to be rich. Although most people think being rich is about having money, rich is a description for everything but money. Rich relationships lead to much more than money. They lead to success, fulfillment and wealth."

As you probably expect there are a few common sense points associated with interpersonal competence too. Understand yourself. Think about what makes you tick. When you are working with someone else, think about what makes him or her tick. If he or she is different from you, decide what you need to do to be better able to communicate with him or her. Second, do things for other people — and don't keep score. Good things will come your way, often from unexpected sources. Build relationships by being willing to do for others whether or not they are willing to do for you. Finally, when you are in conflict, look for where you agree with the other person. Use these small places of agreements to build a mutually acceptable resolution to your conflict.

That's my four ingredient secret success sauce.

- Clarify What Success Means to You
- Commit to Taking Responsibility for Your Success
- Become Self Confident
- Get Competent
    - Create Positive Personal Impact
    - Become an Outstanding Performer
    - Become a Dynamic Communicator
    - Become Interpersonally Competent

As you've seen, it's applied common sense. The secret in creating your own success sauce lies in how you combine these four ingredients into a zesty, robust concoction that will lead to your professional success. I can help you create your personal and unique success sauce. I'll bring the ingredients; you bring a burning desire to succeed. Together we'll whip up a kick ass sauce that will put you on the road to personal and professional success.

If this common sense approach to career and life success appeals to you please get in touch with me for a free, no obligation coaching session. I'll spend some time answering your questions. You'll get a chance to see if I am the right coach for you.

I Want YOU...To Succeed

48

Learn more and get some great free success helpers:
http://BudBilanich.com/success.html

Chapter 6: The Coaching Relationship

Coaching is a profession of love. You can't coach people unless you love them.

Eddie Robinson

Unlike many professional relationships, coaching is comprehensive. As a coach, I am not only trained in techniques to help you discover the answers to your unique challenges; I am ethically committed to a completely confidential partnership with you — one that helps you achieve your goals.

In other words, I won't come to our relationship with a preconceived idea of what is best for you. Rather, I will gently probe to identify your desires and goals, and then dedicate myself to helping you fulfill and accomplish them.

You can expect me to be honest and give truthful feedback about all aspects of the coaching relationship. Sometimes, this feedback might include some observations that you won't like to hear. Don't worry though, I am in skilled in the use of language and am able to deliver my thoughts and observations in a constructive, helpful manner.

You should expect, and even demand, that I provide you with feedback, both positive and negative, during our sessions. In many ways, this feedback will be the most valuable product of our coaching relationship.

I will remind you of your progress, endorse who you are, empathize with you when you fall short, and celebrate with you when you achieve one of your milestones. You can count on me to be on your side 100% of the time.

Working with a coach is not always easy. When the time is right, I will make big requests of you — bigger than you might make of yourself. I'll do this because it will help you realize that you are capable of much more than you give yourself credit for. Coaching can be disconcerting, as I'll ask you to move out of your comfort zone. As uncomfortable as this may be, it is effective. And I'll be there to support you as you move into uncharted territory.

In short, you can expect that our coaching relationship will be characterized by mutual respect, support, truthfulness, honesty, growth, and fulfillment. This might sound unrealistic at first, but these are essential elements in any effective coaching relationship.

Chapter 7: People I Have Helped

Make sure that team members know they are working with you, not for you.

John Wooden

"If only Bud Bilanich could be cloned and sent to help every person who wants to become a personal and professional success! There is a reason why he is called 'The Common Sense Guy.' While there is no shortage of 'gurus' and books that rely on gimmicks or the newest fad to increase personal and professional growth, Bud helped me by using his wits and his common sense. Thirty minutes into our first call, he was able to help me quickly recognize what was holding me back. Then he helped me come up with solutions that really worked for me. He didn't stop there. He followed through by helping me develop my personal step-by-step success plan. He checked back with me to help me stay on track. He didn't quit. Bud made the whole experience enjoyable with his upbeat personality and his humor. He was genuinely interested in your success and it shows. If only there were a thousand more just like him."
 – LW - Marana AZ

"If you want to succeed in your life and career and need some help, Bud Bilanich is the man for you. I highly value his common sense approach to business and life. I have found again and again that Bud Bilanich is effective, helpful, relevant, and overflows with common sense. He really cares about me as a client and is genuinely interested in my success. He has a knack for telling the truth about a situation without being painfully blunt. My wife said she noticed a difference in me after only a few calls with Bud. I would highly recommend him to anyone needing a coach in their life."
   – LAP - Statesboro, NC

"Bud Bilanich's common sense approach, sense of humor and good nature make him easy to work with. He doesn't talk down to you no matter how much knowledge he has. He is truthful and helpful, not hurtful. He amazed me with his listening skills and by how quickly he zeroed in on exactly what help I needed the most. He went the extra mile to help me. He really made me feel I could succeed, and I have!"
   – LG - Orlando, FL

"I was really struggling in my job and in my life. A friend suggested I get in touch with Bud Bilanich. That call changed my life. He helped me zero in on what was holding me back and came up with simple steps I could take to get moving forward again.

"Bud's ability to inspire you both personally and professionally is astonishing. He is one of the most positive, upbeat individuals I have come across in all of the workshops and seminars I have attended in my career. He helped me go from a complete lack of self confidence to feeling great about myself. If you want to succeed, you need to attend one of his workshops, engage him to coach you, or at the very least, read his books on success."

   – KG - Madison, WI

"I was struggling in my job. I couldn't seem to get ahead. Then I met Bud Bilanich. He explained his 'secret success sauce' recipe to me and showed me how to apply it to my life and career. If you are looking for a coach to lead you in the right direction and help you become the best you can be, you need to seek his help. Bud is a phenomenal human being who has had years of experience in career and leadership development. His unbiased feedback and thought provoking insight helped me get the promotion that eluded me for so long. Bud can help you fix your problems and take you to that next level of professionalism and success."

   – JB - Adrian, MI

Learn more and get some great free success helpers:
http://BudBilanich.com/success.html

"Bud Bilanich is a coach who really cares. He can lead you to right where you want to go. He is amazing. He is honest, caring, genuine and can make such a difference in your life. I know because he has made a huge difference in mine. A couple of months after I started working with Bud, people at work began saying that I was a different person. I've received two promotions since I started working with Bud."
   – CW - Los Alamos, TX

"There is no better coach than Bud Bilanich! This caring and compassionate man is simply the best there is! He's always willing to help. He is positive and upbeat. Not only is he just about the most honest and thoughtful guy I've ever had the pleasure of working with, but he's got the credentials to back him up. His experience really shows. Dr. Bilanich always focused on my achievement. He spent the time and took the extra steps that helped me get the job and promotion I so dearly wanted. He is an inspiring person and coach. Thanks Bud."
   – FE - Richmond, IN

"Bud Bilanich is an awesome career and life coach. In fact, his name suits him very well. His attitude and method of coaching was like having a buddy that came alongside me and provided common sense strategies for my professional and personal development. The greatest thing about Bud is his ability to be truthful without being hurtful or harsh. He always seemed to know the right thing to say. He was genuinely interested in my overall success. I know this because he was always willing to go the extra mile and do whatever it took to encourage and keep me motivated and moving forward in my life and career. He helped me remain positive by making me feel that I can do whatever I put my mind to do. He never talked down to me and is very compassionate and caring. I would recommend him to anyone who would like to have a positive, well respected, common sense success coach."

– DR - Sheridan, WY

"Bud Bilanich is a well-spoken, talented, and personable coach, speaker and writer. I learned a lot from his seminars and enjoyed his book, *Straight Talk for Success*. He believes that we all have what it takes to succeed. That's why I chose him as my coach. He was willing to do whatever it took to help me succeed. At first, I was leery about building a business because I was unsure about leaving the security of a good job. I questioned my knowledge and my reasoning. Bud helped me face my fears. After working with him, I believe that I am able to face my challenges and succeed."

– DG - Palm Bay, FL

"It's too bad that everyone can not have a coach and role model like Bud Bilanich. While he has many worthy credentials, it is his common sense approach that makes him so unique and helpful. He is a great coach and role model; and a great person."
– CH - Roseville, MI

Chapter 8: How to Contact Me

It's OK to let down your guard and allow your players to get to know you. They don't care how much you know until they know how much you care.

Pat Summitt

If what I have to say interests you, please get in touch. The best way is via my office phone 303.393. 0446. I am in the Mountain Time Zone in the USA (GMT + 7). The best times to reach me via telephone are between the hours of 9:00 and 5:00 Monday through Friday. If I am unavailable when you call, I promise to get back to within 24 hours. In most cases, I will call you back in two hours or less.

Email is also a good way to get in touch: Bud@BudBilanich.com. I will respond to emails within 24 hours also.

You can also use snail mail — but it takes longer and is not as personal.

My office address is:

> Bud Bilanich
> The Common Sense Guy
> 191 University Boulevard, #414
> Denver, CO 80206 USA

I offer a free 30 minute coaching session. In this session you will have the opportunity to experience me in action before deciding if I am the right coach for you.

Chapter 9: Resources

"The greatest university is a collection of books."

Thomas Carlyle

"Today, the greatest university is a collection of books and a high speed internet connection."

Bud Bilanich

There are zillions of books on personal and professional success. I have bought and read a lot of them. Here is a list of books (arranged alphabetically by author) to which I find myself returning over and over. They are a good resource for anyone interested in personal and professional success – and my gift to you. Check them out, you'll be glad you did.

This isn't a real bibliography, as it contains only the book titles and author's names. However, in this day of Amazon.com and Barnes and Noble.com, I think that's all you'll need to find what you're looking for.

Ouch! That Stereotype Hurts; Leslie Aguilar

Listening; Madelyn Burley-Allen

Career Distinction; William Arruda and Kirsten Dixson

Difficult People at Work; Arthur H. Bell; Dayle M. Smith

Executive Charisma; D. A. Benton

The Job Search Solution; Tony Beshara

Basic Black; Cathie Black

Goal Setting for Results; Gary Ryan Blair

The One Minute Apology; Ken Blanchard and Margret McBride

Ten Things I Learned from Bill Porter; Shelly Brady

As a Gentleman Would Say; John Bridges and Bryan Curtis

How to Be a Gentleman; John Bridges

High Impact Public Speaking; William T. Brooks

First Break all the Rules; Marcus Buckingham and Curt Coffman

Now, Discover Your Strengths; Marcus Buckingham and Donald O. Clifton

The Secret; Rhonda Byrne

How to Win Friends and Influence People; Dale Carnegie

The Excellent 11; Ron Clark

Learn more and get some great free success helpers:
http://BudBilanich.com/success.html

Soar With Your Strengths; Donald O. Clifton and Paula Nelson

Rules for Renegades; Christine Comaford-Lynch

Daily Reflections for Highly Effective People; Stephen Covey

Seven Habits of Highly Effective People; Stephen Covey

The 8th Habit; Stephen Covey

Write to the Top; Deborah Dumaine

The Fine Art of Small Talk; Debra Fine

Getting to Yes; Roger Fisher and William Ury

Poor Richard's Almanac; Benjamin Franklin

The Law of Achievement; Kathleen Gage, Lori Giovannoni

101 Ways to Captivate a Business Audience; Sue Gaulke

The Little Black Book of Connections; Jeffrey Gitomer

The Little Gold Book of YES! Attitude; Jeffrey Gitomer

The Little Green Book of Getting Your Way; Jeffrey Gitomer

The Little Platinum Book of Cha-Ching! Jeffrey Gitomer

Learn more and get some great free success helpers:
http://BudBilanich.com/success.html

The Little Red Book of Selling; Jeffrey Gitomer

The Little Teal Book of Trust; Jeffrey Gitomer

Creating WE; Judith Glaser

Social Intelligence; Daniel Goleman

A Grammar Book for You and I...Oops, Me! C. Edward Good

A Gentleman's Guide to Appearance; Clinton T. Greenleaf III

A Gentleman's Guide to Etiquette; Clinton T. Greenleaf III

I'm OK – You're OK; Thomas Harris

Face to Face Communication for Clarity and Impact; Harvard Business School Press

You Can Excel in Times of Change; Shad Helmstetter

Hermanisms; John Herman

The Innkeepers Tales; John Herman

Think and Grow Rich; Napoleon Hill

Radical Careering; Sally Hogshead

The Nibble Theory; Kaleel Jamison

The Little Book of Confidence; Susan Jeffers

Stress Breakers; Helene Lerner and Roberta Elins

The Six Fundamentals of Success; Stuart R. Levine

We Are Smarter Than Me; Barry Libert and Jon Spector

Make Peace With Anyone; David J. Lieberman

Conversations With Millionaires; Mike Litman and Jason Oman

How to Be a Master Networker; James Malinchak and Joe Martin

Success Starts With Attitude; James Malinchak

Turbo Charge Your Career; James Malinchak

The 17 Essential Qualities of a Team Player; John C. Maxwell

There's No Such Thing as "Business Ethics"; John C. Maxwell

On Being; Peggy McColl

The Proven Secrets to Smart Success; Peggy McColl

Your Destiny Switch; Peggy McColl

Talk Ain't Cheap...It's Priceless; Eileen McDargh

I Wish You Would Just...; Todd McDonald and Kyndra Wilson

Be Your Own Brand; David McNally and Karl D. Speak

Effective E-Mail Made E-Z; Verne Meyer; Pat Sebranek, John Van Rys

Flipping the Switch; John G. Miller

QBQ: The Question Behind the Question; John G. Miller

The Brand Called You; Peter Montoya

The Personal Branding Phenomenon; Peter Montoya

Please Just Don't Do What I Tell You; Bob Nelson

Cool Careers for Dummies; Marty Nemko

212; S. L. Parker

Crucial Conversation; Kerry Patterson, Joseph Grenny, Ron McMillan, Al Switzler

The Power of Positive Thinking; Norman Vincent Peale

The Brand You 50; Tom Peters

Essential Manners for Men; Peter Post

C and the Box; Frank A. Prince

Manners That Sell; Lydia Ramsey

You're Hired; Bill Rancic

How Full is Your Bucket? Tom Rath and Donald O. Clifton

101 Great Ways to Improve Your Life, Volumes 1, 2 and 3; David Riklan

Business Etiquette; Ann Marie Sabath

Love is the Killer App; Tim Sanders

Fierce Conversations; Susan Scott

The Little Instruction Book of Business Etiquette; Valerie Sokolosky

How Outstanding People Manage Time; Erika Steffen and R. James Steffen

Difficult Conversations; Douglas Stone, Bruce Patton, Sheila Heen

The No Asshole Rule; Robert I. Sutton

The Rules of Life; Richard Templar

The Rules of Work; Richard Templar

The Power of Nice; Linda Kaplan Thaler and Robin Koval

The Top Performer's Guide to Change; Tim Ursiny and Barbara A. Kay

The Top Performer's Guide to Conflict; Tim Ursiny and Dave Bolz

Learn more and get some great free success helpers:
http://BudBilanich.com/success.html

Start Right, Stay Right; Steve Ventura

Start Right, Lead Right; Steve Ventura

Working Relationships; Bob Wall

From Day One; William J. White

The Angel Inside; Chris Widener

Wildly Sophisticated; Nicole Williams

Above, I shared some of my favorite books on personal and professional success with you. Here is a list of web resources, blogs, e-zines and web sites that I find myself returning to over and over again. I guarantee that you will find interesting and helpful career and life success guidance on each one of them.

www.GetMotivation.com, published by Josh Hinds

www.SuccessTelevision.com, published by Helen Whelan

www.AudioMotivation, published by Andy O'Bryan

www.GMarketing.com
www.GuerrillaMarketingAssociation.com
www.gmarketing.com/radio, all published by Jay Conrad Levinson

www.Powerfull-Living.biz, published by Lorraine Cohen

www.JimRohn.com/ezines.asp, published by Jim Rohn

www.MikeLitman.com/ezines.php, published by Mike Litman

www.Destinies.com, published by Peggy McColl

www.BrianTracy.com, published by Brian Tracy

www.KevinEikenberry.com/uypw/archive.asp, published by Kevin Eikenberry *www.simpleology.com*, published by Mark Joyner

www.justsell.com

www.salesdog.com

www.WritingHelpTools.com/blog.html, published by Shaun Fawcett

www.naphill.org, published by The Napoleon Hill Foundation

www.ChrisWidener.com/ezinesignup.asp, published by Chris Widener

www.ThinkRightNow.com

www.InstantInnerPower.com, both published by Mike Brescia

www.YourSuccessStore.com, published by Ron White

www.KnowMoreMedia.com

www.VitalSmarts.com/CrucialSkillsArchive.aspx, published by Vital Smarts

www.WalkTheTalk.com, published by the Walk the Talk Company

www.EverythingCounts.com, published by The Goals Guy

www.MrPositive.com, published by Dave Boufford

www.ThinkTQ.com

www.SalesCaffeine.com, published by Jeffrey Gitomer

www.RonKarr.com, published by Ron Karr

www.CorporateClassInc.com, published by Diane Craig

www.SelfGrowth.com, published by David Riklan

www.DaveNavarro.com/Wealthblog, published by Dave Navarro

www.MindTools.com, published by James Manktelow

www.ReachCC.com, published by William Arruda

www.DebraBenton.com, published by Debra Benton

www.DebraFine.com, published by Debra Fine

www.MannersThatSell.com, published by Lydia Ramsey

http://BobSutton.typepad.com, published by Bob Sutton

www.emilypost.com, published by The Emily Post Institute

www.goalsguy.com, published by Gary Ryan Blair

http://blog.JackHayhow.com, published by Jack Hayhow

www.ThePowerOfNice.com/index.php?/nice_blog/, published by Linda Kaplan Thaler and Robin Koval

http://SandersSays.Typepad.com/sanders_says/, published by Tim Sanders

www.SusanJeffers.com, published by Susan Jeffers

www.RWUniversity.com, published by Joe Martin

www.essentialmessage.com, published by Michel Neray

www.Peace-Together.com, published by Bobbi Benson and Joseph Bernard (I like their message)

www.Chipotle.com (I like their food and their philanthropy)

and of course,

www.SuccessCommonSense.com, published by Bud Bilanich

www.CommonSenseCoach.com, published by Bud Bilanich

Questions for Bud

* _____
* _____
* _____
* _____
* _____
* _____
* _____
* _____
* _____
* _____
* _____
* _____
* _____
* _____

You've read the book.

You have your questions.

Now is the time to act.

**Schedule a free
30 minute coaching session.**

Call Bud at 303 393 0446

Or...

**Send an email to
Bud@BudBilanich.com**

**Suggest some good days and times
for Bud to schedule your FREE
coaching session.**